GRIDS OF CONSCIOUSNESS UNIFICATION

COMPENDIUM OF LIVING UNITY CONSCIOUSNESS

PRINCIPLES & PRACTICES

ALIGNED COLLECTIVE SERVICE TO GOD AND HUMANITY

GROUP **R**ESPONSIBILITY **I**N **D**IVINE **S**TRUCTURE

AUTHORS
GRACE MARAMA URI AND JAMES GERMAIN URI,
DOCTORS OF COSMOCRACY

EDITORS/AUTHORS - FOURTH EDITION
ANGELA MAGDALENE URI AND JAMES GERMAIN URI
DOCTORS OF COSMOCRACY

THIS PUBLICATION IS COMPLIMENTARY IN PERSPECTIVE WITH

COTC GRIDS ACCORD SEMINAR™

churchofthecreator.com/participation/cotc-seminars

Church Of The Creator®

churchofthecreator.com

COTC PUBLICATIONS & PRODUCTIONS

P. O. BOX 157, ASHLAND, OREGON 97520 (541) 776-9191

FIRST EDITION

© 1984 TE-TA-MA TRUTH FOUNDATION - FAMILY OF URI, INC.

FOURTH EDITION
EXTENDED CONCEPTS AND CONCEPTUALIZATIONS
ISBN: 0-9760287-9-4   ISBN13: 978-0-9760287-9-6

CHURCH OF THE CREATOR®   DIVINE RIGHT ORDER®   URI®
HUMAN SOFTWARE FOR BEING®
ARE REGISTERED TRADEMARKS OF   TE-TA-MA TRUTH FOUNDATION -
FAMILY OF URI, INC., ® © 1984 - 2019
ALL RIGHTS RESERVED.

Contents

G R I D S OF CONSCIOUSNESS UNIFICATION 1

Editors Preface 5

Foreword 6

Introduction 8

Chapter I 11

Chapter II 15

Chapter III 19

Chapter IV 23

Chapter V 29

Appendix 32

    Consecration 41

    Dispensation 42

    Sacred Mandate Certificate 43

    Structure & Plan 44

    Purpose & Function 44

Venues of Participation 46

    COTC Circles Of Light 46

    COTC Seminars 46

    COTC Associate Ministers 46

Support System Nurturing Human Evolution 48

Office Of The Christ 48

Cosmocracy 48

Chronology Of Human Evolution 49

O R D E R within Chaos 67

Glossary Of Terms 70

Divine Right Order® 73

Administrative Authorities 77

Office Of The Christ 77

Christ Michael - Order of Michael 77

Shekinah - Holy Spirit - Divine Mother 78

Order of The Mother - Sisterhood of Mary 80

Melchizedek - Order, Brotherhood, Priesthood of Melchizedek 80

Orders Of Whole Light Beings 82

Plate 1. Triune Energy GRID - TRINITIZED FUNCTION 86

Plate 2. ACTIVATION OF SEED CRYSTALS - THE HEART FUNCTION 87

Editors Preface

Expressions of this publication are **Aligned** to **G R O U P Consciousness GRIDS** as now established on planet Earth and it's Systems. Written in 1979 - 1980, to bring about better understanding of the reciprocal flow of collective energy and living experiences. The words written have been authored by the individuals, as representatives of example, while living as ONE BODY, within a "Family Of Ten," the prototype Melchizedek Community Of Light™, "Ship Terra," Prospect, Oregon, 1979 - 1985.

This compendium issued through Church Of The Creator,® is a Conscious Directive within and through the **Office Of The Christ**, a tool to bring about the unification of Christ Expressions into ONE COLLECTIVE ASSEMBLAGE.

Foreword

The scope of this publication is specific. **Principles and Practices** when applied, evolving synergy within collective configurations of human beings. Guidelines germane to spiritual, physical, extended family, associations, organizations and institutions. **HOW-TO** steps of building up solidarity cognizance, facilitating, encountering unity with one another and the **Whole of Creation**.

An Operators Manual for piloting, navigating, experiencing collective Multi-dimensional Merkabah Vehicles within *GRIDS of Consciousness Unification* for Members, Ministers, all human beings living upon planet Earth, Church Of The Creator.®

Principles and Practices to establish resonating frequencies of Light within those present, to interface with the *GRIDS of Consciousness Unification* anchored within our soul, DNA, Aligned to the One Creator Source.

Principles and Practices to synchronize, focus effort, step-by-step co-creation within Multi-Dimensional Estates. Co-creating, restoring our planet Earth, Humanity, to the Divine Blueprint, Manifesting Heaven on Earth.

Principles and Practices of collectively asking for guidance, our part, next steps to be taken.

Alignment - "Consciousness attunement within and through the Office Of The Christ to that which is highest and for the greatest good of the Whole; a specific agreement as to time, place, action, activity, etc., agreed upon in support of unified action requiring conscious effort to fulfill by more than one individual."

Like any vehicle manual, this publication won't take you anywhere. With any vehicle, a plan, study, may bolster subjective advancement; however, we must build it, get inside, take a ride to fully understand its use. Before we start it is wise to agree upon purpose, designate individuals to be at the helm, an initial direction, and then launch on our journey. In this instance, we start as human beings, drawn together, connecting in a circle, choosing to act together, unanimous Accord. Choosing to **Align** our efforts in the arena of our chosen purpose, interface with guidance available within a collective **Merkabah Vehicle of Light**.

The start button is reaching agreement to unify in consciousness, as equals at the table, letting go of judgment, **"Behold the Perfection"** of each one present.

Utilize operational Principles and Practices enabling everyone opportunity to express, tune in to the frequencies of *GRIDS of Consciousness Unification* and get help from our **Counterparts**, waiting for us to inquire. In the asking, from within the Collective Merkabah, Pillar of Light, the Divine Guidance, Miracles waiting for each Child of God, our Divine Inheritance become self-evident.

Enjoy the journey!

Introduction

GRIDS of Consciousness Unification already exist. Access is a function of the collective consciousness of those present. There is a threshold frequency of unified energy required to interface multidimensionality.

We pay tribute to those individuals who have come to that one conscious place of understanding; service to Creation, the choice is made in support of the Whole, to utilize the highest possible function of Our God Essence. Through self-realization each recognizes that we must participate collectively with those of like heartmind, dedication and purpose, therefore, amplifying to the maximum, our individual effort in service, becoming a cell (Realized Self) in the

Redemptive Christ Body, within and through the **Office Of The Christ**.

In having reached that place of accord, the primary motivation of each one being ready to do what is "...**highest and best for the Whole**..," many personality concepts will **Release** from all involved. This is a mutual process and once accomplished, within the space made together, a quantum leap in consciousness understanding occurs, where each one will expand and become representative of the **Whole**, as is needed to affect the Divine Plan. This is **Cosmic Christ Consciousness**, **G**roup **R**esponsibility **I**n **D**ivine **S**tructure, **G R I D S**.

Key words in **bold** type are defined within the Glossary or other sections, or references at the back of the book

God
Represents
Our
Unified
Parts

URI

Chapter I

G R O U P - God Represents Our Unified Parts

Let us recognize those here gathered in consciousness. First and foremost we reside at ONE, in the presence of our Parent Creator Source. This is in truth the point of our joining and in forever holding this awareness in our consciousness; we keep the avenues open, ready to receive the support available, within and through the Office Of The Christ.

Church Of The Creator® is Commissioned, established, and anchored through the Group Consciousness GRIDS of the Holy Trinity, Divine Deity. Those individuals attracted to participate in any capacity of expression through this Church and its Associate Ministers have on another level chosen and are already functioning in group consciousness. The tools contained in GRIDS will assist in bringing that choice into the fullness of outer manifestation.

As a point of beginning, each individual member becomes a unifying compliment by making the necessary choice and effort in this plane and dimension.

The compound overall interest and desire should always be unification.

Utilize written guidelines for collective participation. If not already in existence, create the structure that will bring the purpose and function or your collective work into a written document.

Define the unifying elements of your participation, each unto the other and always abide with that Accord. The words set the pattern in this plane and dimension of your Collective Vehicle and are the place through choice of mutual agreement to which all have pledged support, your common bond, each unto the other and therefore the Whole.

If you find in your growth as a Unified Functioning Body that you have gone beyond the consciousness of your foundation stone, then make the expansion needed. Revise, expand and anchor your collective goals and guidelines.

We recommend you become familiar with the terminology, publications and organizing documents of Church Of The Creator.® They have been established in practical application on the principles as set forth in GRIDS and are the common threads throughout the weave.

As alternatives present themselves in opportunity of co-creation, always choose the Group Vehicle and insure the results of your inspiration.

The totality of a collective work is not the sum of the parts. Each one's effort through unification and singleness of purpose expands the Whole in many multiples of the individual's contribution. The results of our collective effort is multiplied thousands upon thousands of times as we move in Group Unity within and through the Office Of The Christ.

Each individual, need remain in consciousness unified with the Whole, or the Whole suffers a loss in functioning capacity in the same amplified proportion.

The Whole functions as Wheels within Wheels, not as parallel Wheels or as the same Wheel in two or more places.

It is important to recognize that true Group Movement by Christed individuals working together with an outer organization, cohesive in purpose and function and in alignment to man's law and Divine Law is only now being re-established on this planet. Change being created by your conscious collective effort is of vast significance.

Representatives
Entrusted
Serve
Perfectly
Our
Natural
Synergism
Inherently
Birthed
In
Loving
Indwelling
Trinitized
You

Chapter II

RESPONSIBILITY -

Representatives **E**ntrusted **S**erve **P**erfectly **O**ur **N**atural **S**ynergism **I**nherently **B**irthed **I**n **L**oving **I**ndwelling **T**rinitized **Y**ou

All responsibilities are co-created through free-will choice and agreement. We each choose and have been chosen.

It is our responsibility and solemn pledge to the ONE Living God, The Holy Trinity and Each Other to manifest as the Redemptive Christ Body, each supportive of the Whole, all portraying through example the Living Word Made Flesh.

If each one is not working for the Whole, then automatically, as a matter of Divine Law, they are working against the Whole. This principle applies on all levels of functioning groups. At home, at work and play.

It is our responsibility to choose always to remain unified.

Those warring factors, areas of duality consciousness, must by agreement to the "Christ Pact" bring about a Consciousness Amnesty and learn to move together Peaceably.

To accomplish this simply stated goal will require all the collective strength, experience and tools available and it is to be recognized that it requires the energies of the Group

Consciousness GRIDS as now established within and through the Office Of The Christ.

Our responsibility is collective and can only be realized collectively, in Christ Accord.

When the individual member through unilateral choice is expressing or seeking guidance from the consciousness of individualized service once having been infused through the Group Consciousness GRIDS, they have neglected their responsibility to the Whole and can become subjected to the duality broadcast of paradox.

Physical vehicles, when joined in this plane and dimension and aligned in all consciousness planes and dimensions within and through the Office Of The Christ, serve as a buffer mechanism for each one present. The responsibility therefore is to utilize the Aligned Group Vehicle thus the expression and guidance received will automatically be aligned to that which is highest and best for the Whole.

It is our responsibility to each other to support all parts of our collective vehicle by performing and carrying out the agreements made. It is also our responsibility to Behold Perfectly each one entrusted by choice and agreement to act for and represent the Whole, whatever the functioning level, or combination of the parts.

It is the responsibility of the Members, Officers, Councils, Boards, those Spiritually Affiliated, to stay appraised of and function within the law, those created by man and God.

Recognize that through perfect beholdance in affirmation and use of the transcending tool, Divine Right Order® that automatic change will occur.

In compliance and support of man's law from the Group Consciousness GRIDS of Divine Law, evolution must manifest.

As we raise our heart together, in Praise and Prayer, resonating with the Whole, singularly and collectively we strengthen our responsibility in Glorification to Our Parent and in fulfilling that TRUST PLACED IN US.

Interrelating Nucleus

Chapter III

I N - Interrelating Nucleus

Knowledge of the Christ Group has been gifted to this planet and its systems. Those asking are receiving recognition of their Responsibility to come together as a Collective Vehicle, a Family, aligned within and through the Office Of The Christ. Church Of The Creator® through its Associate Ministers, Affiliate Auxiliaries, COTC Circles Of Light,™ is a Vehicle to bring this knowledge forth as Wisdom, through the Heart, the Feminine Principle and Balance, I N LIVING EXAMPLE.

To assure that the Interrelating Nucleus, the Divine Spark within each of us, has the opportunity to manifest collectively, there are simple awareness, tools and alignments that all functioning groups may utilize.

On coming together in any combination for any purpose, first, stabilize in that quiet place, align through all planes and dimensions and call forth the perfection and purpose for your joining.

Recognize the vibration and presence of our supportive counterparts, within and through the Office Of The Christ, and hold within this alignment as you move in co-creation.

Do not move into areas that are counterproductive to the specific purpose for which you are representatives in the now. Re-stabilize when needed.

On completion of your joining, close, heal and seal all loose ends. This encourages a clean release. Be aware of reopening the membrane through social discussion following this process.

An agenda is a useful tool. Support and information to the one responsible for its preparation is necessary.

Gatherings may be stabilized through focus of a chairperson(s) and perfect beholdance of that one(s) as they act in the highest and best interest of the Whole.

Utilize a recorder to hold the highlights of gatherings and bring forth your written record (minutes, journal, log, etc.) as soon as possible in order that the collective consciousness has a precise reference upon which unified action can be founded.

If it is not perfectly clear as to what is to be accomplished through those assembled, collectively attune and ask for guidance.

The guidance received will be highest and best for the Whole as long as the questions and vibration of those gathered are maintaining in that unified Group Consciousness GRID. If the question asked, or the motivation is individually oriented, there will be no connection to the Group Consciousness GRIDS and hence the guidance will inevitably be from another estate of consciousness.

The following is suggested during your gatherings and collective attunements:

FOCUS only on areas pertinent to the joining. Attune only to those matters that are in correct timing and the responsibility of the ones gathered.

Frame questions from the collective view and compound interest of those assembled, in support of what is highest and best for the Whole.

State the question without inclusion of even the most subtle content that would support pre-conclusion as to outcome, conceptualization of outcome, or personality orientations.

When clear direction is established and supported by those gathered, then request specific guidance relating to:

What is the next step to be taken?

Who is/are the one(s) to act (have the authority) for the Whole and in what part and combination?

Is there an aligned timing for completion?   All other discernment's needed at this time of attunement?

Timing for the next attunement or gathering relating to this specific matter?

In the living application of these principles, this cohesive Love, Collective Movement in Trust of Heart and Mind, will bring about the recognition of the Indwelling LOVE and PURITY of the CHRIST VIBRATION, where we all met, within and through the OFFICE OF THE CHRIST.

Dedicated
Individuals
Viably
Interconnecting
New
Endeavours

Chapter IV

D I V I N E - **D**edicated **I**ndividuals **V**iably **I**nterconnecting **N**ew **E**ndeavours

Our Parent Creator Source is a Trinitized Expression of ONE, evolving infinite personalities.

In outer expression this is the Spiritual-Physical Family, Mankind's Divine Lineage, His alignment to the Hierarchical Family Tree, the overcontrol synthesizer of the Divine Blueprint.

Group Consciousness GRIDS are trinitized function and expression, through all planes and dimensions.

On all levels we are never working alone. It is of paramount importance that this awareness conscientiously be with us at all times, individually, collectively, spontaneously and organizationally.

This is the example of DIVINITY, THREE IN ONE. Within and through the Trinitized *GRIDS of Consciousness Unification* the individual is always asking for the Whole and therefore always receiving for the Whole.

In this estate, there is a continuum issuing for Divine thought forms and pictographic infusion, combinations of probability and possibility, causation relationships in human expression, the next step (s), in manifestation of the Divine Plan. These areas of inspiration in uplifting Humanity's expression can only be received and activated through the collective energies of Cosmic Christ Consciousness.

The individual attuned to Group Consciousness GRIDS becomes the recipient of Spiritualized human conceptualization, buffered by the supportive energies of the collective.

Once received and anchored, the unilateral conceptualization can be brought into the consciousness of the Whole through Group Attunement. Witness as to timing and filtering in the combined energies of unanimous support through conscious choice, the expression therefore becomes balanced within the Whole, thus establishing the New Order Of All Things.

GRIDS is a tool to manifest the Divine Example through common sense application, now activated and utilizing mankind's desire to move together as One Consciousness Body.

Mankind over the centuries has had the innate desire to live in a Utopian Society, yet has failed to realize that ideal. The greatest blockage and obstacle has always been in personal release of objects into the impersonal Love of the Christ Vibration, which once embraced helps heal and seal forever those areas of consciousness responsible for selfish motivation and warlike personalities.

Trinitized consciousness automatically activates understanding that all thoughts – all things are merely energies at different vibrational levels, wholly manifesting as they are created, whether objects or words. All however emanate from, return to, and in truth belong to the Godhead.

Group Consciousness GRIDS enfold the understanding of Guardianship, a Divine Responsibility if right-use of the God Essence Energy, whatever the form. This understanding when applied as a Divine Responsibility within and through the Office Of The Christ the instrument to see made manifest Heaven on Earth.

At the point of embracing as truth that all energies and objects belong to Our Parent, the individual becomes cognitive of their Divine Birthright. As a Son or Daughter they are also inheritors of the Whole of our Parent's abundance.

Each one is directly accountable to the Father for the right-use of the God Essence entrusted to their individual guardianship. How that guardianship is administered has a vast effect upon the Whole.

Once guided and choosing in the highest and best interest of the Whole to transfer guardianship to the collective vehicle, an individual need only to complete the act through the written word of legal title to fulfill the commitment. Then and only then does this become a topic and concern of the collective, through Group Responsibility for right-use.

That action of transfer automatically connects the gift through Divine Right Order,® to a timing and outcome aligned to what is the highest and best for the Whole.

These understandings and principles apply on all levels of human expression, individual, family, group, commerce, governmental, etc. and are the KEY to bringing the material plane into balance of Divine Trinitized Expression.

When exemplified on any level, these principles automatically synchronize and mesh within and through the Office Of The Christ, and the efforts and expressions activated receive the amplification of that ONE Unified Body.

DIVINE

Dedicated **I**ndividuals **V**iably **I**nterconnecting **N**ew **E**ndeavors

RIGHT

Redemptive **I**nfusion **G**od's **H**igher **T**ruths

ORDER®

Overself **R**estoration **D**egeneration **E**ternally **R**edeemed

S trength
T enacity
R esiliency
U nending
C hrist
T ransformative
U nctioned
R edemptive
E volution

Chapter V

STRUCTURE - **S**trength **T**enacity **R**esiliency **U**nending **C**hrist **T**ransformative **U**nctioned **R**edemptive **E**volution

Redemptive Evolution Perfect STRUCTURE begins and ends in the relationship expressed within and through Trinitized Trinity.

STRUCTURE is relationship that manifests strength greater than the sum of the parts.

STRUCTURE is organization, through which, by mutual agreement, Church Of The Creator® functions as a Whole, within the Whole.

STRUCTURE is the GRID of our fabric as we co-create within the Divine Tapestry.

Church Of The Creator® is a function aligned to reciprocal resonance of the color coding and harmonics within and through the Six Pointed Star Grid, perfect in its Pattern.

Each member becomes a Living Brick, tempered, resilient, within the STRUCTURE, a thread within the cloth, the internal weave.

Each thought, each word, each action, each combination has a direct effect upon the qualitative strength, texture and integrity of the collective co-creation.

We are always in Church. The Church is in US. From the perspective of this plane and dimension, our lives our daily living, are the basic unit of the STRUCTURE.

Once brought into the weave, the Body, the Temple, will show the results of the movement of the parts. As the individual consciousness functions within and through the Office Of The Christ, the STRUCTURE of the Group Consciousness GRIDS strengthen and the auxiliary expressions, organizations, spiritual/physical families gain strength in their part, of seeing made manifest a New Heaven on Earth.

To strengthen the STRUCTURE it must be exercised as a Whole, in attunement with the Group Consciousness GRIDS. This requires conscious effort, tenacity and practice through application of the principles and tools as expressed in GRIDS.S

Recognize that each time there is a joining (individual in prayer, Church Service, COTC Circle of Light,™ Board or Committee meeting) that co-creation is in process within the STRUCTURE.

Each gathering has its own unique purpose and function within the resonating vibrational harmonic of the Divine Tapestry. With practice the correct combinations will bring the perfect inner pattern of the weave to outer manifestation. The parts once amalgamated are relative to the Whole, functioning organs, perfect integral parts.

Unification in outer expression of the Redemptive Body Vehicle can only be experienced through participation within the Collective Energy Grids. This experience of unity is not at all what the individual consciousness projects and conceptualizes. In attaining harmonious balance the heart is witness to its purity and truth, for in essence it is Unconditional Love.

Those ones, our counterparts, the Seventy-Two (72) Brotherhoods, the Seventy-Two (72) aspects of the Order Of The Mother, The Sisterhood Of Mary, who function within and through the Office Of The Christ stand collectively ready to support us, Church Of The Creator,® as a GROUP and through use of the Group Consciousness GRIDS now established, their Light and Wisdom, through our choice, can be amplified in the QUICKENING AND INFUSING OF THE HIGHER TRUTHS FOR THOSE READY TO RECEIVE THEIR DIVINE INHERITANCE!

Make no mistake in understanding, our counterparts are dependent upon and limited by the free-will choice of those ones who said they would remember the COVENANT and move into COHESIVE ORGANIZED GROUP EFFORT.

Appendix

Humanity must move beyond **thinking** about our oneness, **talking** about our personal spiritual experiences, our unique individual circumstances, move beyond the intellectual concepts, emotional, feeling bodies, baggage of the past. We can choose collectively to act upon our shared convictions, focus upon unity, whole of humanity here and NOW.

Sounds simple, but to do so, we must be prepared to face our fears, doubts, whatever separates us in consciousness, remnants of duality.

When we are brave enough to sit in a circle, choose to quieten the mind, thinking, talking, and connect holding hands something happens. A few deep breaths will bring our consciousness to the place and space of NOW, our oneness becomes tangible within the heart function. We will recognize that everyone present has value, unique perspective, is important, a co-creator, in whatever the collective purpose requiring group effort. From within that quiet space, **WE** may utilize mechanisms existing within us, choose to **Align**, synchronize our human spiritual/physical family, group configuration with forces that sustain and uphold the **Whole of Creation.**

The **Aligned Amplified Field of Light** will surface within group dynamics all aspects of consciousness blockage. Energy shifts within a specific circumstance, topic, difference of opinion, (**the symptom**) may be perceived, out-picturing as conflict, anger, guilt, alienation, victim/abuser, any aspect of duality consciousness, separation. Those perceiving the energy shift, step up, ask for a time out, pause, identify, isolate the miscreated energy from the individuals out picturing the separation, acknowledge and let go of the symptom. Unify in asking to be shown the root of the consciousness blockage, relevant event(s) within the memory membrane, any trigger mechanisms. Once identified, acknowledged, healing may occur, blockage will **Release,** our vibration will **Stabilize** and our ability to remain unified strengthened.

After reading this publication, **if you choose to give it value; organize a gathering** with others in addition to yourself. Create a proposed agenda, narrow or broad in scope. Remember, our **Counterparts**, those who have supported you for the entirety of your life walk, complementary guides of other invitees will be listening, and they will be present at the appointed time. **It is the invitation**, "Let's come together, to focus our effort, Align to the Greater Picture and Plan for Humanity, Creation" that activates the multi-dimensional participation.

Initially in applying these Principles and Practices, recognize individually and collectively, human beings have been beleaguered by phobias- "an exaggerated usually inexplicable and illogical fear of a particular object, class of objects, or situation."

When phobias surface, show themselves, stall, divert, takeover the collective focus of your activity, stop, **let go of the symptom - Stabilize** and **Release**.

Before, during and after group gatherings utilize the Principles and Practices of *GRIDS of Consciousness Unification*.

To assist discernment, review of a few phobias within our collective consciousness operating within old patterns of separation, conflict, chaos, warring factors of duality consciousness, may be of assistance.

FOJI - fear of joining in and **JOMO** - joy of missing out; **Theophobia** - fear of gods or religion; **Ecclesiophobia** - fear of churches; **Religiophobia** - fear or hatred of religion, religious faith, religious people or religious organizations. **Atelphobia** - fear of not being "good enough." The list is endless, the whys of the mind that we feed our God Essence, keeping them alive. Fear, separation, bigotry, polarization, in all its forms is self-evident within the chaos out picturing on planet Earth.

Trinitized Light Infusion is the causal source of the purification of human collective consciousness now occurring on Earth. Like a pot of gold the more Love, Light and Peace added to the caldron, the more the slag comes to the surface, easily seen and identified. Once seen, identified, we may collectively choose to **Release** the symptoms, clear the fear at the root level, experience individual and collective healing within **Program Adonai Tsebayoth**.

In the past, prior to the **Dispensation of 1969**, no matter how we might try, individually or collectively, humanity could not be at peace, due to outside interferences, overlays, mechanisms affecting the inhabitants of Earth. Since that time through support of the Heavenly Hierarchies, arrival of hundreds of thousands of old Souls embodied on Earth, Divinely Commissioned representatives have collectively removed all aspects of the prior interference. Karmic debt has been balanced, lifted, through transmutation of miscreated energy, within the whole of our collective memory membrane. Our Galactic Citizenship was re-instated in 2006, and warring factors prohibited from entering our time/space continuum.

Previously there was truth in the statement "the Devil made me do it." Today that reference to outside interference influencing our ability to live peaceable, harmoniously on Earth is an excuse. The same goes for any other "reason" that the mind can come up with that we use when choosing to do something, act upon an old pattern, that within our Heart, we know is not the best choice. When we establish within our lives, a spiritual/physical family interfaced with the *GRIDS of Consciousness Unification*, our other arenas of individual engagement will be stabilized, buffered through the support of our immediate spiritual/physical unified GRID. The best choice in every situation requiring our decision in the NOW

35

made easier to discern. Excuses for not choosing, not acting upon the best for all of us, will fall away no longer needed.

J.K. Rowling reminds us "**Fear of a name increases fear of the thing itself.**"

Initial attempts to utilize these GROUP Principles and Practices may surface other phobias within the invitees. They may surface, be discerned, as "reasons" for non-participation within collective configurations. Trust that the individuals ready to move collectively, interface within *GRIDS of Consciousness Unification,* will respond to the invitation, be present, and participate.

There is a comfort box within our mind. We can lock ourselves within our own experience, limit and avoid interaction with others. We may place others in the same box of preconceived judgment, expectations, action and reaction, our own creation, for our own comfort, to avoid dealing with the symptoms that we know will surface.

Example? Are we more comfortable, if we give the same beliefs, convictions, a different name, within the mantel of different protocols? "The core difference between religion and spirituality is that religion presents you a set of beliefs, dogmas and "holy men" as intermediaries between you and (Holy) Spirit (however you may name it); while spirituality promotes your individual autonomy in defining and connecting to Spirit as it fits your heart and mind..." quote from a coach, one who will help you learn to meditate, guide you, coach you on living, but not call themselves a "holy man" or "intermediary."

Can we be comfortable with belonging, claiming our membership, participating with others "...joining in principle and witness..." to common convictions, while still expressing within other denominations, non-denominations, structures, dogma, ritual, meditation, or individual relationship with the unified field that sustains all, the Whole of Creation?

Fear makes us uncomfortable, and can be released, no longer needed within our relationships on any level, any place on Planet Earth.

Tested method that works - group sessions. Just sit down together with those you trust, all of it will be exposed, can be healed, taken care of within the process of **Release**, within the GRIDS, through the gift, dispensation, Decree of **Divine Right Order**.®

The **Decree Divine Right Order**® is also an automatic filter that assists in the perfect mix of participants, those responding to your invitation. Who is not in the circle of action is just as important as those who are. It is the quality, frequency of harmony that is most important, not the number of participants in this plane and dimension, estate of consciousness.

Beholdance - The human estate of consciousness, Principle and Practice that **replaces fear** with **Trust, Balance, Co-creation within the GRID.**

The other-dimensional participants, our **Counterparts** have the capability to adjust, work through the representatives present, as we and they Amplify and Infuse Divine Light, for who we are and who we represent, to the rest of Humanity, implement Divine Law. Through those choosing, therefore chosen, everyone represented will receive the results of efforts to unify. We can choose to limit the results of our effort, if we allow our consciousness to slip below the weave, embrace fallen thought forms that tell us we are working alone, just human beings, unable able to directly support, affect others, unworthy, not qualified to be Divinely Commissioned.

When is the last time you sat down with your physical/spiritual/extended family, at home, at work, or at play to adjust, enhance unity? When is the last time you participated within a meeting that someone called, for the purpose of, as defined in the Glossary, **Alignment**?

You are already individually Aligned with the Creator and Creation. It is the very essence from whence we came into Being, "I am That, I AM." We are Divine, Children of God, a fact, not a function of free-will choice from this end of existence. You can believe it or not, deny it or not, it is what it is, REALITY.

Action is the key, to collectively interface with *GRIDS of Consciousness Unification*. Invitation sent, agenda delivered, participants present in the now - where do we go from here?

Suggestion - utilize the light frequencies already anchored, activated and operational.

The **Sacred Mandate** when spoken together, through the Word, the Breath, will automatically bring your collective vehicle into **Alignment**, within the greater picture and Divine Plan. Review the **Sacred Mandate**, a tool to synchronize with others on Earth, "Treatise Of Joining in Principle and Witness," "...dedicate our physical embodiments...," linked to universal forces, from Earth to the "....One Creator Source..." activating assistance through the Decree, "Divine Right Order.®"

Individually, download, print and sign the **Sacred Mandate Certificate**. In man's law, it creates a contract, firmly anchors collective intent, who, where, how, to accomplish a specific goal, "...Manifestation of Heaven On Earth..." connecting you with others already living within the Accord.

Within the group setting, find and anchor a name for collective intent, purpose for gathering, goal, write it on the document, and ask everyone, as an Addendum, your part, within the Greater Accord, collectively sign, date the document. This action further synchronizes your collective mission as a wheel within wheels of Co-Creation.

Two historical examples of the **Practice - collectively anchoring Divine Law within man's law**, through documents, action of collective signatures, aligned within

Divine Timing. Review the seed for the United States of America, the *"Mayflower Compact."* More mature after nurturing, tending of the seed planted, *"The Declaration Of Independence."* Signatures make a difference. The very thought of signing requires discernment, knowing it has consequences in man's law, it also surfaces phobias, fears, rooted individual experience, the past, "how will this affect me?"

History is loaded with examples where the Divine Vision was given, the concept seeded, but never coming to fruition due to fear - "how will this affect me?" - real or perceived. That part of the Divine Plan stillborn, waiting for other parents, somewhere else, some other time.

Utilizing the Principles and Practices of *GRIDS of Consciousness Unification* is not a teacher/student, expert/layman, lecture or other solo concert event. It is conscious unified collective entry into a Pillar of Light, a Light Elevator, from Earth to Home.

To begin the process of **Alignment**, co-creating a Merkabah Vehicle of Light, **Stabilize** - "Centering-in to the quiet place within one's Christ Beingness; harmonizing all parts, each part in support of the others; at the moment one is "stable" there is harmony throughout all of the bodies; bringing the Inner into the Outer; coming together, joined in a circle, (holding hands, eyes closed) establishing the energy flow of ONENESS, and setting the vibration for the forthcoming movement as a group."

In addition to the *Sacred Mandate*, the **Consecration** is suggested as a group prayer, to establish unity within your circle. Spoken collectively, Aligned within the Divine Program - **Adonai Tsebayoth**, program of the **Mother, Daughter, Sister, Mate, the Feminine Expression, Balance of the Heart.**

Consecration

We Recognize This Whole Planet Earth

To Be A Living Monument In The Glory Of The Father

Dedicated By Michael, The Bestowal Christ Son Jesus

To The Divine Mother Essence, The Holy Spirit

By Whose Holy Breath It Is Sustained

- So Be It and So It Is -

[Opening Article of the Ecclesia Magna Charta, Article I, Organizational Document, Church Of The Creator® © 1984.]

To Heal and Seal the Merkabah Vehicle of Light as we prepare to serve within our individual expressions of life and living, consider speaking together the ***Dispensation***.

Dispensation

This Church, This Functioning Body Decrees

That As Long As It May Serve This Planet, This Humanity

So Therefore Are We Prepared

To Be The Instruments In Which To Serve

The One Living God,

Who Has Placed A Trust In Us

- So Be It and So It Is -

Amen, Amen, Amen and Amen

[Ending Article, *Articles Of Faith & Constitution*, TE-TA-MA Truth Foundation - Family Of URI, Inc. All Rights Reserved. © 1976]

Sacred Mandate Certificate

Sacred Mandate
Treatise of Joining In Principle and Witness

Church Of The Creator®
Supports The Family Unification of Mankind
In All Aspects Of The Whole.
We of Like Mind Join Harmoniously In
Oneness, Knowing That There Is Only
One Creator Source.
The Many In One,
Dedicate Our Physical Embodiments
To The God Expression In Form,
Bringing Forth By Example
To This Planet Earth
Love, Light and Peace.
Therefore Once Decreeng
Divine Right Order®
In All Thoughts – All Things,
Our Universe Automatically Aligns Into
Manifestation of Heaven On Earth.
Through The Priesthood of Melchizedek
We Are One In The Body Of Jesus Christ.
As Above So Below

Signature

DIVINE RIGHT ORDER © 1977, 1982 TE-TA-MA Truth Foundation-Family Of URI, Inc. Church Of The Creator® All rights reserved. URI

Structure & Plan

"In that we recognize this Whole Planet Earth to be the Father's Church and that each Christed Being is in themselves a complete Temple, a Home, a Tabernacle made unto the likeness of The Creator, a House of God, so therefore in coming together to move in like-mind each representative then becomes an individual living brick, a stone, in Church Of The Creator.®

Each one adds their part by expanding and living through the Redemptive Body of the Christ Son and progresses daily in the bringing forth into outer manifestation the Spiritual Gifts of Shekinah, Sacred Sciences, through the Feminine Principle and Priesthood. This is the Daughter's offering in Regenesis to the Whole, through service and within the Divine Blueprint of the Father's Plan, the Descending/Ascending Vehicle of Mankind - the Family." [Article V of the Ecclesia Magna Charta, Organizational Document of Church Of The Creator® © 1984.]

Purpose & Function

"Church Of The Creator® shall provide the vehicle and vibrational grid to attract those of common understanding, desiring to bring release of Spiritual Relativity, and the Anchoring in of Spiritual Reality and Restoration of the Common (Co-Man) Law, as exemplified through the understanding and pronouncement of our Beloved Brother, Christ Jesus, "Love Ye One Another as I have Loved Ye Also."

Church Of The Creator® shall provide that place within, where each may have the opportunity to express the Perfect Principle of Love - that retribution of such will be the instrument and tool to see manifest Heaven on Earth.

Church Of The Creator® is the Vanguard, Spiritual Consciouship of Michael, aligned to the Order, Brotherhood, Priesthood of Melchizedek in compliment with The Orders Of Whole Light Beings to bring forth Melchizedek Communities Of Light,™ Melchizedek Academies Of Light,™ Universal Centers to enlighten, expound God's New Truths.

Church Of The Creator® shall provide that each and every one may bring about a physical conceptualization of their own interpretation of the God Essence and the opportunity to Glorify in God, singularly or collectively, as they choose to express.

Church Of The Creator® shall function through all its parts, its members, each supportive of the Whole, all portraying through their Golden Example and Sacred Mandate The Living Word Made Flesh." [Article VI of the Ecclesia Magna Charta, Organizational Document of Church Of The Creator® © 1984.]

Venues of Participation

COTC Circles Of Light™ are an expression of Individuals composed of COTC Associate Ministers, Members, and guests. COTC Circles Of Light™ provide a Place & Vibrational GRID wherein individuals "Joining in Principle and Witness," on a regularly scheduled basis, participate and demonstrate the Principles & Practices, within communities, local expressions of service to humanity.

COTC Seminars™ vary in length to compliment the circumstances of those hosting, facilitating and participating. Experiential Collective Participation, recommended for all Ministers, Candidates for Ordination, invited guests, or anyone interested in experiencing the Principles & Practices, of *GRIDS of Consciousness Unification*.

COTC Associate Ministers are those choosing, commissioned and witnessed to be the Instruments to Mandate and infuse the Higher Truths to this Humanity, to bring forth into manifest state the Sacred Sciences of the Holy Spirit Shekinah - AMEN - AMEN; and in proclaiming these truths shall HERALD, AFFIRM, TEACH, and SANCTIFY in preparation and Celebration of that which is descending unto and through the Redemptive Vehicle of the Bestowal Son Jesus, the Office Of The Christ.

COTC Path Seminar™ and **Priesthood Of Melchizedek Seminar**™ may assist individuals choosing, being chosen, to become a Candidate for Ordination, Commissioned, Ordained, within the Ministerial Position, COTC Associate Minister. It is a Spiritual calling, commitment to live a Collective Covenant &

Pact as the People of Light, the True Israel, demonstrating by example the Principles and Practices of the Church.

® Trademark of TE-TA-MA Truth Foumdation-Family Of URI, Inc.

URI - IRU
United Estates of Consciousness
I am That, I AM

Support System Nurturing Human Evolution

Office Of The Christ - "...coordinated by the Orders of Michael, Metatron and Melchizedek, has the responsibility and administrative authority in the Hierarchy of Heavenly Government, to bring about the necessary purification and consciousness evolvement on this planetary sphere and its fallen universe. Known and unknown avatars of Humanity, in all fields and disciplines, have had representatives of their Lifestreams in consciousness within this collective effort."

Cosmocracy

"Co-joint Democratic Healing and Sealing the Planes and Dimensions into a Unified Body. Cosmological Democracy; an integral planning in coordination within the Brotherhoods, step by step locking in process. The counterpart in the Electro-Magnetic Shield surrounding us in our many Universes. Externalizing the COMMUNITIES OF LIGHT by the ORDER OF MELCHIZEDEK in attunement, accordance, and principle of PHASE 2 by the FEDERATION and GALACTIC COUNCILS in our Pact and Covenant to Our Parent Creator to fulfill the cause-effect of Man's Destiny."

Chronology of Human Evolution
There is only NOW

Human sensate experience of time/space as we have known it is RELATIVITY; forward-backward, up-down, good-bad, us-them, life-death, paradox, duality consciousness.

REALITY, the other side of the tapestry, the causal matrix of human experience, is without duality restriction, always evolving, adjusting, in the NOW, as a **Whole**.

Human Beings are co-creators, participating through free-will choice, in manifesting our collective experience within third dimensional relativity, now transitioning to fifth dimensional life and living, as we complete the Alpha-Omega Program. "Then I saw a new heaven and a new earth..."

This *Chronology of Human Evolution* assumes the above premises are true. It is broad in scope, respective prior and current **Human Consciousness Evolution Programs.**

Human history, time/space linear events may be organized like storyboards, delivering the concept for various scenarios within the human drama. We live within an interactive universe co-creating, filling in the details between major quantum shifts, from one evolutionary sequence to the next. This analogy is offered to assist the reader in understanding the author's perspective. The reader is not being asked to believe anything. This quick journey through human evolution is offered to get on the same page, how we got here, the message within the chaos.

The reader is being asked, to find that quiet place within yourself, your process of recognizing Divine Truth. Discern what resonates as truth already within you. No analysis, no debate, no why or why not, no proof necessary, because the Heart Function within each human being resonates with fundamental truth. The Sophia is within us. Trust the subtle promptings of your heart.

In the beginning, the First Creational Thought Seed Adam, Creation happens.

Species on Earth come into existence, evolving chemical, biological diversity, including primates. Evolving also is the consciousness operating the species, instincts, feelings, electro-chemical brain activity, until such time, experience has reached conditions fertile for installation of the "missing link." Consciousness evolution reaching a point of choice where consideration of another being, their needs, takes precedence over one's own survival.

Love has blossomed. The Creator adds a gift, a thought-adjustor, soul, find a word you like, a new Spiritual addition to the evolving biology that makes us Human Beings.

By design we are **Composite Beings**, physical/Spiritual entities, existing before and after what may be perceived as human life and death.

Mortal humans, inside the paradox of relativity are evolving individually at various rates as we mature, some ahead, some behind, many in the middle.

"A disturbance in the Force" perceived, but not discerned by humans takes place in more evolved Estates of Creation. There is a rebellion, Angelic Orders take matters into their own hands, exercise their free-will and set about tampering with the Creator's Creation. Let's reference this event as "The Fall."

That affected the mortals living on planet Earth, as well as a lot of other places. This happened a long, long, long, time ago.

We are asking you to yield to a few concepts, assumptions, simply for the sake of moving on. Please set aside individual beliefs relative the details, arguments that will not change or override the final destination, only delay arrival at the solution to getting beyond our current chaos on Earth.

The Creator/Source/Unified-Field/God/Force, is ONE with everything, but expresses through differentiated forms. At the root of differentiation, ONE expressing in three parts, lets reference this as **The Divine Blueprint, The Family**, The Father, The Mother, The Son, The Daughter, The Sister, The Brother, the Mates of Our Being, The Holy Trinity.

This basic unit, the family, exists throughout creation, travels in all planes and dimensions. Two parties unite, creating the physical component, the DNA, sustained by the human mother until birth. The third party, God, Creator, Holy Trinity, adds the spiritual component of our composite nature, extending, propagating within the Divine Blueprint, the Divine Essence that makes us Human Beings.

For the biological component entry to our individual experience is through the womb route, the Vesica Piscis. The consciousness, the spiritual component arrives through the first Breath, the Holy Spirit. We are composed of ascending, descending components evolving through experience, Eternal Lifestreams of the One Source. Within mortal experience, buffer mechanisms suspended conscious awareness of prior existence, the long term memory for most of us, is not accessible, although encoded within our DNA. Baby human beings experience everything as new. Small "independent human beings," who need a lot of help from someone, love and care necessary to continue the sensate journey, another paradox of our existence.

So collectively, after eons of time our human families are evolving. Due to "The Fall" our Divine Blueprint, is corrupted. Our Spiritual Circuits are overlaid, setting up internal loops of regression causing a lot of pain, suffering that does not assist in evolution of our character, the ascending aspect of our Being. Not our fault, we were "kidnapped," and it became easy to believe that it always was and always will be more of the same.

Always adjusting, the Creator designates trusted children in multi-dimensional realms to clean up the mess. Appointed administrators, locally, collectively named, the Office Of The Christ, Department of Restoration and Redemption.

It is determined that a cleansing is necessary. The event is witnessed, within multiple cultural remnant records, written on parchments, and in stone. Let's use a Christian record, or substitute the one that you are familiar with, reference the story of the flood, **Noah and his family**. Remember Noah asked others to help, shared the message delivered by **Uriel**, "get ready a flood is coming," but his peers wrote him off as a bit delusional, rejected the messenger and the message.

"Why so many problems on earth if there is a Divine Blueprint, if we are a Divine Creation?"

It is a function of human free-will choice. No matter how many times humanity chooses to reject the Creator's Avatars, Ambassadors, Messengers sent to help us, like a good GPS system, the Creator doesn't call us names, scold or banish us from Creation when we refuse the suggestions. The Planners just recalculate, provide alternative routing. Eventually once we realize we are lost, a few of us do accept and implement the guidance. Through the few, we all get the benefit, eventually evolving. **In Reality, that is a Divine Law**, "...one can and does represent the Whole,..." when Divinely Commissioned.

Within human records we find evidence of **Programs** designed to correct aberrations within human evolution due to

"The Fall." Programs planned and delivered within and through **The Office Of The Christ.** Programs long before the recent calendar reset of year zero, human BC - AC time management. Programs of Divine Intervention evolving collective consciousness, demonstrating fundamental change, that adjusts our expressions, eventually affecting all people of the Earth, all aeons within linear time/space. Consciousness upgrades that do not dissolve evaporate or vanish, even when we try to erase, delete from the record events amplified through consciousness Infusion of Light delivering. Programs that feature a main character, a supporting cast and appear periodically within human history.

Planned evolution, delivered through human beings with ascending evolving souls and/or spiritual components of descending highly evolved beings. Individuals Divinely Commissioned prior to embodiment to seed our collective consciousness. They are Aligned, live encoded scenarios seeding, upgrading network protocols, patterns, pathways, within our collective consciousness and the rest of us catch up as fast as we can, that is, choose to.

"**Program**: noun 1. a set of related measures or activities with a particular long-term aim. 2. a series of coded software instructions to control the operation of a computer or other machine. Verb 1. provide (a computer or other machine) with coded instructions for the automatic performance of a task. 2. arrange according to a plan or schedule."

Long after Noah, his family and the creatures departed the Ark, cleansing accomplished, the Planners set the stage, prepare human lineage for further adjustments. Reference **Abraham**, and **Melchizedek** - "...born without father or mother." Place an emerald green light around that second name. Someone of record, not using the womb route to arrive, without the restrictions of suspended consciousness, a not so human Composite Being sent to advise.

Fast forward, the next leading character arrives under mysterious circumstances. An oppressed mother takes a big risk with her much loved baby. Enter **Moses**, supporting cast Aaron, Pharaoh, Miriam, others. Delivered through the drama a **Message**, - "...you are loved and have a Heavenly, Father who will lead you to the land of milk and honey. I am his spokesperson, He will set us free." Demonstrated through events, sufficient evidence that Moses indeed was getting a lot of help from somewhere, not so easy to write off, even for Pharaoh. Let's call this this series of events by the Planners name - **The Father Program.**

Now free, Exodus complete, new problems soon surface, events not within the script of the Planners. Out from under the oppression of Pharaoh, many human beings were not happy. "Not fast enough. Not how we thought it was going to be. We want more, now! Moses is missing, gone somewhere.

Let's re-create the old after all it's what we are used to, no unknowns." So when Moses descends to deliver the **To Do Tablets** they had to be broken. The supporting cast had recreated the old "many gods" within the New Program, One God, our Parent, and truncated the planned outcome.

Recalculation, adjustments, request to Moses, go back up the mountain for the **Don't Do Tablets.** Then deliver to the representatives of change, followed by 40 years of wandering to overcome the consequences of rejecting the guidelines, within the first set of Tablets. **Human free-will choice creates the delay**, not the original Plan encoded within the Divinely Commissioned Cast, prior to arriving on Earth.

Fast forward about 1500 years plus or minus human error. Once again it's not looking so good on Earth. The Roman Empire is interacting with keepers of the Law, the **Covenant of The Father Program - There is Only One God.** The remnant records, Ten Commandments, second set of Tablets, Ark of the Covenant, the law, the Zohar, the **principles**, are intact, **practices** maybe not so much.

Reset, Zero the Calendar. Send the Angelic Messengers, make appearances, witness the early arrivals, **The Son Program** is unfolding. Enter John the Baptist, Gabriel, Mary, Joseph, Uriel and the main character Jesus, Yosef (Joseph Ben Joseph), multiple support cast. **Of note deserving more recognition**, repeatedly deleted from the record, the women supporting and **Beholding the Perfection** of the main character, a heart function.

The message, not only do you have a Father in Heaven that loves you, but, like me you are sons and daughters of God. You are Divine Beings, Children Of God and about to receive your **Divine Inheritance, Everlasting Life, a New Order of Being, New Heavens and New Earth.** You are co-creators with me and our Heavenly Father. Primary suggestion, principle, example lived "...Love one Another as I have Loved you..." Good News indeed!

Let's look for truth, refine discernment within human interpretations of events, satiate the -Why? - incessant inquiry of the human mind. As parents and/or children reflect upon, discern, what kind of Planners, Father/Mother, would send their son on a mission with the **intent** that he would be rejected, tortured, crucified? **Was it the Plan or human rejection of the Plan?**

Consider the nature of the switch without an override, no work-around for those serving the Creator, **human free-will choice**. It's binary, for or against, my will or Thy Will, often the cause of delay in human evolution.

In the biblical story of Jesus, within three years of the official start of his public ministry, witness by John the Baptist, and the Anointing of the Holy Spirit, things were not going so well.

Analogously, if religious/spiritual genre is not within your own arena of conscious participation search out the beginning of what you believe was a quantum change for the good of all humanity. Most likely you will find rejection, resistance to change. The greater the Truth, greater the change, the greater the resistance, rejection, at great personal cost for the messenger, main character and cast.

Any quantum "break from the past," within every venue of human expression, was planned, commissioned within and through The Office Of The Christ. Not by chance, but planned. Spiritually Commissioned Beings, arriving, experiencing human/mortal realms, delivering by example, knowledge, techniques, designs, extraordinary performance's, formulas and theories, ahead of their time to inspire us, encourage us to break from the past.

Finishing a drama with terminal affliction has embedded many a message within our Collective Consciousness. Scenarios that frequent our aggregate cognizance until we comprehend the message, discern the principle, implement the practice and give thanks for the messenger.

Within **The Son Program** review carefully the scene in the garden of Gethsemane. Use the Bible or read the lyrics from *Jesus Christ Superstar*. The Divine Plan when issued did not contain the scenario about to take place. It was known possibility, a probability to be avoided. But the Light Infused Truth He delivered, surfaced fear of change greater than human consciousness within the time/space of his life walk was willing to accept, choose, implement, within our human family. Resistance to change rooted in fear of letting go of old patterns, traditions, authority, and power, truncated the planned outcome.

Recalculation, alternative routing, rewrite, scenes, scenarios that would not go away, seeding the evolution that would follow. The rewrite required agreement of some human beings within the cast. His human free-will choice to follow the rewrite or as a highly evolved Creator Son just exit the drama. Same can be said for the cast member known as Judas, he had a very difficult part, only now being comprehended as necessary, something he was asked by the main character Jesus and agreed to do.

Rejection of elements of the Plan may come from within the cast of Spiritually Commissioned characters, those who said they would execute the agreed upon plan, before physical embodiment. Planning within a realm of harmony is one thing, but setting foot on the ground, executing the plan is another.

Within **The Son Program** following his example within the density of human consciousness at that time precipitated consequences. Tangible direct consequence for anyone even associated to the main character, His demonstrated Principles and Practices of unconditional love and compassion.

Consider one example of cast member rejection, human re-write that caused great delay, misconception, overlay of the Truth - **Divine Principles and Practices of The Son Program.**

Review the record of how the main character treated women. At that time all women were at best second class citizens, valuable and necessary chattel. Over and over, He demonstrated that women were not only co-creative equals within the arena of pro-creation, but **their Spiritual Component was of the Heart**, of a different nature. He demonstrated that they were not only necessary for the human DNA family, but that He was dependent upon their unconditional love and Beholdance to fulfill His Mission. Who was at the cross? Who was the first believer? To whom did He first appear after His Resurrection? Who did He instruct to tell the Apostles who were hiding, that He was out and about as promised?

Why then, for the last couple of thousand years was the yoke born by the women at that time, still upon the backs of the Mothers, Daughters, Sisters, Mates, still existent on Earth today? Cast rejection of the example lived. The male Apostles, created a major rewrite of the plan. They were jealous of the women, how Jesus treated them. The men decided it wouldn't work, wouldn't be accepted. So the women were written out of the script as co-equal in all aspects. The women Apostolic Core was not given credit, accepted or allowed their participation as co-creative equals.

How much faster would we have progressed collectively, had the women been allowed as co-creative equals? Probabilities and possibilities of the Planners Plan, truncated through human free-will choice.

Only now in the current **Program Adonai Tsebayoth, Program of the Holy Spirit Shekinah,** is the Mother, Daughter, Sister, Mate being reinstated to their rightful position as co-creative equals, balance of the heart, to the male/mind.

Marker, 1980, the Energy of the Divine Feminine, the Holy Grail, held in England, Glastonbury, anchored there after the masculine Apostles rejection of the women, is retrieved and reactivated in the New Jerusalem the USA. That story is full of detail, but not now, not here.

The evidence is everywhere. Change is at hand within the male dominated overlaid institutions of religion, government and commerce. Institutions now being reorganized, rebalanced, reset, through the women standing up, saying and acting upon the realization that enough is enough and getting some support, by those recognizing its their time to be front and center.

Other signs of where we are headed, the Spiritually Commissioned inspired artists, producers, authors, delivering the same message, placing before us a smorgasbord of probabilities and possibilities, of Human Evolution. Movies like "2001," "Contact," "Interstellar," "Close Encounters of the Third Kind," "The Matrix Series," "Star Trek," are examples of conceptualizations preparing our collective consciousness for what is happening NOW on Planet Earth.

Search the global computer network. Time has been accelerated, compressed. Almost instant information retrieval, of historical documents, film, videos, and music, almost everything is online, including a lot of human miscreation. Search "Spiritual," "Evolution," "12 Strand DNA Activation," "Enlightenment," "Heaven," "Consciousness," "Ascension," "Indigo Children" "Near Death Experience," "Cosmic Christ Consciousness," etc. and you will find thousands of publications, titles, arriving from other realms, the Planners call it the **Dispensation of 1969**.

Recent predecessor, the **Dispensation of 1932**, released to the public, humanity, ancient wisdom previously preserved within Wisdom Mystery Schools. Preserved through Ascended Master-Disciples transmission, apprenticeship, archives of ancient wisdom. Search "Blavatsky," "Ouspensky," "James Churchward," "Ballard" a few of many Divinely Commissioned human beings bringing information into the public domain, on the bookshelf for anyone asking. "Seek and you will find" made easier, quicker, no apprenticeship or entry fee.

Search on information systems now operating on earth, "advancements in science and technology for the last 100 years compared to the timeline of all human existence." Zoom out, backwards in relative time, human understanding is no longer limited to short focus instruments centered upon our mortal existence, a recent quantum leap. Most humans accept, believe, incorporate the reality that we are not alone, isolated or understand fully our own history, those previously inhabiting the planet, let alone intelligent beings beyond and within our own galaxy. New theories abound for creation of the known universe, time/space no longer separate, but interrelated, no longer duality concepts. Multi-dimensional consciousness realms are present, operational and we are beginning to understand who we are and from whence we came.

Zooming in, scientific applications of knowledge gained are genome mapping, genome sequencing and the "80% junk DNA" turns out to be the memory membrane of our biological ancestors, still not entirely accessible unless the proper ID/passwords have been issued from somewhere, that some of our fellow human beings seem to possess and know how to use.

Thousands of authors, Divinely Commissioned Souls are delivering the new. Enhancing every detail of how creation is built, who we are, where we are going, what is available to break from the past. In their own words a few of our fellow humans bringing change, share their discernment relative the source of their inspiration.

Nicola Tesla, "Every living being is an engine geared to the wheel-work of the universe. Though seemingly affected only by its immediate surroundings, the sphere of external influence extends to infinite distance..." "...My brain is only a receiver, in the Universe there is a core from which we obtain knowledge, strength and inspiration. I have not penetrated into the secrets of this core, but I know that it exists."

Wolfgang Amadeus Mozart, "...I have never written the music that was in my heart to write; perhaps I never shall with this brain and these fingers, but I know that hereafter it will be written; when instead of these few inlets of the senses through which we now secure impressions from without, there shall be a flood of impressions from all sides; and instead of these few tones of our little octave, there shall be an infinite scale of harmonies - for I feel it - I am sure of it. This world of music, whose borders even now I have scarcely entered, is a reality, is immortal..."

Edgar Casey "...This is the first lesson ye should learn: There is so much good in the worst of us, and so much bad in the best of us, it doesn't behoove any of us to speak evil of the rest of us. This is a universal law, and until one begins to make application of same, one may not go very far in spiritual or soul development..." "From the subconscious forces, which become universal by the natural laws governing RELATIVITY OF ALL FORCE: whether spirit, soul or physical, and the information is obtained through that connection between subconscious soul or spirit forces as directed, and directed to..."

"If the first woman God ever made was strong enough to turn the world upside down all alone, these together ought to be able to turn it back and get it right side up again." — Sojourner Truth, American abolitionist

Humanity is reaching critical mass within our collective consciousness the quantum leap from me to WE. Collective Transfiguration as a Family Of God. Add your name to the list, ask and receive.

"Incubation - Transformation, Thirteenth Tribe is now Emerging, Yearning, Pulling, Gently, Strong, Our Devotion to Our Parent, Here on Earth, Our Heavenly Home, Holy Trinity, Divine Deity, Hear 'Beloveds Let Us Transcend' "- Grace Marama URI, *Space Of Grace-Parables in Prose, Universal Family* ©1977 TE-TA-MA Truth Foundation-Family Of URI, Inc.

Today we find ourselves individually and collectively in a cauldron of seeming chaos.

O R D E R within Chaos

Requires Spiritual Discernment

Spiritual Discernment is critical to navigate the accelerated purification of humanity. Life, living, circumstances, relationships, ideas, things are not as "black and white" as they used to be...there is a much larger gray area. There is so much going on around us, "fake news", consciously created propaganda (e.g.: "information, especially of a biased or misleading nature, used to promote or publicize a particular political cause or point of view") intended to shift consciousness, cloud our Spiritual Discernment of Truth. The gray area widens, the mind begins to accept consciousness that it once rejected, the clarity of Spiritual Discernment and Knowing can become "blurred." It is imperative we remain within the "Pillar of Light, within and through the Office of The Christ" in every thought, word and deed, 24 hours a day, seven days a week.

How we are using, giving, focusing our God Essence Energy, in thought, word and deed is critical, our contribution assisting or delaying change. Am I assisting or delaying the Divine Plan within this Time/Space continuum, the Ascending/Descending Programs of the Office of the Christ? Ask, review, receive, adjust, use your direct connection to the

Holy Spirit Shekinah for navigation assistance. Keep your GPS - **G**od's **P**erfected **S**ynchronization - switched on.

Individually and Collectively, WE are being called upon to exercise our Spiritual Discernment to navigate through the "eye of the needle," release negative, fallen thought forms. We are being asked to embrace and amplify pure thoughts, Aligned with the Ascended Masters of Light, Angelic Hosts, Heavenly Hierarchy, so former things are no longer called to mind. Your part counts, individually and Collectively we are Co-Creating the New Earth within New Heavens!

Accelerated change continues, through chaos within social, economic, political, government, institutions and geophysical systems on earth, as well as a general feeling of unrest. "There will be weeping and gnashing of teeth," mentioned 13 times in the Bible, referring to the last threads of the dark cabal hanging on as mankind must move through the "eye of the needle", out of the threshold of "lukewarm," and fully don Garments of Light.

Call to Action - "We must be in bodies of Light to be accepted into the Kingdoms of Light." When we are in our Christed Bodies of Light, Spiritual Discernment in this plane and dimension becomes easier in times of chaos and confusion. The "Weave and Tapestry" of creation is multi-dimensional. When we put on, live within the Cosmic Christ Consciousness Garment of Light, the Weft and Weave, the Tapestry of Creation becomes alive. Our Spiritual

Discernment is enabled, activated through the Heart. We can see with new eyes, hear with new ears, know, understand, connect the dots, symbols in our linear life, navigate through the chaos, and remain within the eye of the storm of change on Planet Earth.

We can join with others within the Christ Body, consciously choose to come together Collectively, creating a Merkabah of Light, joining and amplifying our Collective Garment of Light. Unified in thought, word and deed, Spiritual Relativity of 5th Dimensional living becomes Spiritual Reality.

"Make no mistake in understanding, our counterparts are dependent upon and limited by the free-will choice of those ones who said they would remember the COVENANT and move into COHESIVE ORGANIZED GROUP EFFORT." *GRIDS of Consciousness Unification*

AUTHORS/EDITORS
MAY 26, 2019
FOURTH EDITION

ANGELA MAGDALENE & JAMES GERMAIN URI
DOCTORS OF COSMOCRACY

Glossary Of Terms

Definitions supplemental to English Dictionaries, complimentary to understanding being established through living example, Aligned within and through The Office Of The Christ, Order, Brotherhood and Priesthood of Melchizedek, Principles & Practices of the Church.

Recommended as an additional reference is *THE BOOK OF KNOWLEDGE: The Keys of Enoch*, The Academy For Future Science, by Dr. James J. and Desiree Hurtak. Keys Of Enoch® is a registered Service Mark of James J. Hurtak. All rights reserved.

Terms Consciously Established Through Living Example

Alignment

Consciousness attunement within and through the Office Of The Christ to that which is highest and for the greatest good of the Whole; a specific agreement as to time, place, action, activity, etc., agreed upon in support of unified action requiring conscious effort to fulfill by more than one individual. Behold

A state of Being - awareness - an estate of consciousness above the Tapestry; a spiritual attitude that brings non-judgment into our everyday living experience; it is faith and acceptance that what is being Beheld is the very best that can be, within the now of the space-time continuum.

Beholdance

A Christed tool that consciously supports within each one the perfection of the God Essence, irrespective of outer manifest expression; the IMMACULATE CONCEPT.

Beholdance of the Perfect Christ Expression of one another (including one's SELF) establishes:

Trust

Through the positive flow of supportive energy given, each unto the other; the avenue of outer unification is always held open; from the Estate of Oneness, we can transcend any energy experience of apparent separation or disharmony - alienation.

Balance

Through conscious support and trust, discernment can be given and received relative to outer expressions held in the patterning of the old order; thus bringing about release and equalization without ego personality involvement.

Co-creation

In the amplified energies within and through the Office Of The Christ; in trust and balance, the synchronicity of that needed to affect the Divine Plan is aligned as a WHOLE and Beheld by the WHOLE of the Body; thus Heaven on Earth made manifest.

Consciousness GRIDS

The network of Light Energy created and maintained, facilitated by specific consciousness focus; these grids are functional co-creative energies for the manifestation of Divine Truth on Earth, unifying the inner wisdom planes with this plane of reality.

Cosmic Christ Consciousness

A joining through Soul Level agreement of those personalities who have released the individual I AM growth pattern, into the COLLECTIVE I of GROUP UNITY; living in the Group Aspect of the Christ Body; going beyond personal-soul expansion and joining in GROUP to create a synergism of combined spiritual evolvement within and through the OFFICE OF THE CHRIST.

Cosmocracy

Co-joint Democratic Healing and Sealing the Planes and Dimensions into a Unified Body. Cosmological Democracy; an integral planning in coordination within the Brotherhoods, step by step locking in process. The counterpart in the Electro-Magnetic Shield surrounding us in our many Universes. Externalizing the COMMUNITIES OF LIGHT by the ORDER OF MELCHIZEDEK in attunement, accordance, and principle of PHASE 2 by the FEDERATION and GALACTIC COUNCILS in our Pact and Covenant to Our Parent Creator to fulfill the cause-effect of Man's Destiny.

Counterparts

Aspects of our Greater Beingness or Christ Over Self; the Angelic Host supporting the Divine Plan, working with us in this Dimension and in other Mansion Worlds where much inner-plane work is carried out. Human Beingness extends beyond this Third Dimensional Realm through and in conjunction with these Divine Spiritual Expressions; extensions of our Godself, who move in close awareness of our terrestrial endeavorings, ready to protect, support, and guide Mankind toward Universal Familyhood.

Divine Right Order®

A tool of consciousness; an instrument of affirmation which assists in co-creating in the Image and Similitude of our Creator Source; this vibrational harmonic, when spoken, resonates and sets into motion Cosmic and Divine Law, an automatic alignment to manifestation of Heaven on Earth, Highest Truth and Justice for the WHOLE of Creation; through Group Movement in at-one-ment to the Perfection of the Seed Atom of our Parent Creator and asking for Divine Wisdom in being the Instrument that only the Highest Truth manifest in Love; Divine Right Order® shall allow only Truth to manifest, Justice reign supreme, and Love to bring forth Harmony, Liberty, Freedom, and Peace.

Lifestream

Sensitive threads of Light Energy radiating from the GODHEAD, our Creator Source and First Seed Atom; the LIGHT lineage of individual personality expression; the totality of the memory membrane of which each human expression of personality is but a part as expressed in this space-time continuum; the totality of consciousness experience potentially available to any specific embodiment; all human ego-personalities have common origins within the 12 LIFESTREAMS now expressing on this Planet.

Lifestream Representative

Within COSMIC CHRIST CONSCIOUSNESS there are individuals, spiritually commissioned and chosen (by choosing) to represent specific Lifestreams and Soul Groups; these ones act consciously through human free-will choice, their efforts bring about consciousness evolution; some through prior agreement, have embodied, taking on patterns that have originated within the "black cube" energies of the Fallen Hierarchies, so that these distortions of God's original Perfect Plan can be conscientiously turned around creating the space for a New Heaven to manifest on Earth; as imperfect patterns are released, the choice of these representatives opens avenues for greater soul recognition throughout this Planet, its systems and the WHOLE of Human Consciousness is evolved. From COSMIC CHRIST CONSCIOUSNESS, these representatives clearly understand that patterns embraced, unnecessarily, over and over again are traps of consciousness bondage.

Release

Let go and let God; in the aspect of spiritual growth, it is giving up of emotional mind energy; a blockage removal allowing replacement infusion with resonating reciprocal energy and healing by the Holy Spirit; the human ego can manifest in the body as blocked or trapped energy, and "release" removes that blockage; it constitutes handing up and returning of a thought-form which is less than perfect to the Father - a thought that cannot be held in a perfected state of Good; it can be a resentment, an imperfect Beholdance, a traumatic experience of childhood, a fear of something, a habit pattern of less than the highest - these aspects may be latent memory from other embodiments; with this release, trapped energy begins to flow and healing comes to the mind/membrane, the body and to the soul in its progression; a Heart Endowment.

Stabilize

Centering-in to the quiet place within one's Christ Beingness; harmonizing all parts, each part in support of the others; at the moment one is "stable" there is harmony throughout all of the bodies; bringing the Inner into the Outer; coming together, joined in a circle, (holding hands, eyes closed) establishing the energy flow of ONENESS, and setting the vibration for the forthcoming movement as a group.

What is in the Highest & Greatest Good for the Whole of Creation?

This is most important when asking the Father for guidance - the keynote; the criteria for asking; constant attunement, unceasing prayer, through this filter, is the catalyst for best- use of one's God essence Energy; man has evolved as an individual, but in the New Age, the WHOLE is the important factor; it is the coordination of all the parts together that set the vibration on all levels of existence and in all daily activities, thought, word, and action.

Whole

Cosmic Keynote Colors of the Heart/Soul; the experience of the Triune Energies Of The God-Head; the totality of Creation and Creator.

Administrative Authorities
Within our Local Universe

Office Of The Christ

" 'The redemptive Office of divine Light,' encompassing the work of the 144,000 Ascended Masters working with YHWH and Michael through Jesus the Christ for the purification of this fallen universe. This includes all of the Ascended masters who work for the liberation of man throughout the word in all aeons of time." Glossary, *The Book Of Knowledge: The Keys Of Enoch* © 1973, J. J. Hurtak

"The Office Of The Christ, coordinated by the Orders of Michael, Metatron and Melchizedek, has the responsibility and administrative authority in the Hierarchy of Heavenly Government, to bring about the necessary purification and consciousness evolvement on this planetary sphere and its fallen universe. Known and unknown avatars of Humanity, in all fields and disciplines, have had representatives of their Lifestreams in consciousness within this collective effort." *Historical Legacy & Foundations Of The Church* © 1977-2006 TE-TA-MA Truth Foundation-Family Of URI, Inc.

Christ Michael - Order of Michael

"Order of Michael – guards the galaxies from biological-spiritual interference from the lesser forces of light except where necessary to test/train for soul advancement."

"Michael – Eternal Creator and Lord Protector of the Supreme-Ultimate programs of the Lords of Light and hosts in the 'Father Universe'. He ensures that the variations of Light are part of the true spectrum derived from the Lords of Light."

"Christ – 'ho Christos as the Anointed One.' The Father's Son who begins, realizes and consummates the Divine Plan of the Father in the worlds of the Adam Kadmon. Through the incarnate Christ, we assume a new relationship to the Father. By being brothers and sisters to the Son, we are sons and daughter to the Father. Inasmuch as God makes his home in us through the Spirit, we mount to the dignity of Sonship, having the Son himself in us, to whom we are refashioned in his Spirit." Glossary, *The Book Of Knowledge: The Keys Of Enoch,* © 1973, J. J. Hurtak

"In Beholdance and in accordance to Our Creator's Omniscient Wisdom, TE-TA-MA shall manifest in alignment with the Orders of Melchizedek, Metatron, and Michael, the Latter being the Bestowal Christ Son Jesus, and Father in Co-Creation with the Creator Mother Spirit of this Universe." *Articles of Faith and Constitution,* Fourth, © 1977 TE-TA-MA Truth Foundation-Family Of URI, Inc.

Shekinah - Holy Spirit - Divine Mother

"Let it be known that Our Scripture is Our Life, Our Living History dedicated to bringing forth through The Book Of Glories, the Church and Redemptive Body of The Christos, this living monument dedicated to life over death, through the ascending-descending Estates of Consciousness, through the Living Example by experience each unto the other, AMEN. The Great AMEN, the Living Word made Flesh through Our Parent Creator, by The Holy Breath of the Shekinah, Our Divine Mother, is manifesting on this Planet and its Systems in allowance and alignment of The Holy Trinity, The Many in One, The One in Many." *Articles of Faith & Constitution*, Sixth © 1977 TE-TA-MA Truth Foundation-Family Of URI, Inc.

ADONAI TSEBAYOTH - PROGRAM OF THE HOLY SPIRIT SHEKINAH

Order of The Mother - Sisterhood of Mary

"As humanity is collectively transfigured, The Order of the Mother, The Sisterhood of Mary will become manifest in this plane and dimension, part of the Brotherhoods of White Light. While ministering in his garment of flesh, Christ Jesus always beheld the females on equal status, a necessary balance he lived and preached. Through their unconditional love and perfect beholdance, (immaculate concept), deemed necessary to support his resurrection, their dutiful commitment helped accomplish what could not be done through the male apostles. It was with the women apostles, Ministers in the fullest sense of the Word, that he remained, his mother and those other feminine beholders and supporters, who chose to be close to him and form a protective buffer." *Historical Legacy & Foundations Of The Church* © 1977-2006 TE-TA-MA Truth Foundation-Family Of URI, Inc.

Melchizedek - Order, Brotherhood, Priesthood of Melchizedek

"Melchizedek - Eternal Lord of Light. Sovereign of Light in charge of organizing the levels of the Heavenly worlds of YHWH for transit into new creation. Works with Michael and Metatron in the 'rescue, regenesis and reeducation of worlds' going through purification of the Living Light. In the history of the planet, Melchizedek was commissioned (according to the covenant of Enoch) to prepare the true priesthood of 'Sonship' upon a planet for eschatological participation with the Sons of Light."

"Order Of Melchizedek - The Melchizedek Order is after the Order of the Son of God. It governs the quadrants of the planetary worlds where the Adamic seed has been transplanted, administering spiritual things to these worlds. It holds the keys to the opening of the heavens with respect to the contact area on the earth, and has the ability to commune with the celestial communities of the Brotherhoods of Light throughout the father universe coordinating the work of the Christ in the heavens and on earth. The Order is eternal and has foreordained its 'Priests and Programs' before the world was." Glossary, *The Book Of Knowledge: The Keys Of Enoch* © 1973, J. J. Hurtak

"Church Of The Creator® is the Vanguard, the Spiritual Consciouship of Michael, and is in alignment to the bringing forth of the Light Communities and Universal Centers to teach and expound the New Truths through the Order of Melchizedek." *Ecclesia Magna Charta - Church Of The Creator,*® Article IV Section 2, Purpose & Function, © 1984 TE-TA-MA Truth Foundation-Family Of URI, Inc.

Orders Of Whole Light Beings

"Whole Light Beings are "Those entities of Light that exist in pure bodies of energy and travel through the universes by quanta mechanistic corpuscles of Light and move in the midst of man by gravitational fluxline controls."

"Through the Office of the Christ this continued state of soul confusion and inability to connect with "limitless intercommunication" is recognized and compensated for by the human attunement to the spiritual intermediary of the Office of the Christ. The Office directs the spiritual intermediaries assigned to balance the communion between the physical self and the Overself within progressive states of degeneracy. Therefore, the individual can override negative programming through help from the Office of the Christ which is in coordination with the other Whole Light Beings."

"The keys to Future Luminaries are Whole Light Beings who will give Energy Codes for Limitless Intercommunication between Living Universes and 'the Power of Righteousness and Compassion' which holds love-powered radiations together in the cycles of 'The Eternal Inheritance.'"

"From the Councils of Light, the 'Whole Light Beings', emissaries carrying the codes of limitless intercommunications keyed to go from the TAV ת into the JAH יה, the synthesis of all the Light emanations of the Holy Sephiroth giving Divine instruction. Therefore, the future luminaries are those who wear the JAH upon their foreheads for they have gone through the TAV to recognize the end which has no end. These codes are given to the meek and righteous of the Earth who plant their codes by compassion and love-powered radiations." *The Book of Knowledge: The Keys of Enoch*, Key 303 by J.J. Hurtak © 1973

"Because our Purpose in TE-TA-MA is in Singleness of Thought, that of having a vibrational patterning so that those of Like-Mind may and can have a gravitational grid to motivate to, we see ourselves as just that, a giving and receiving of like-life energy patterns or waves, so in joining we are able at this point in time to be a multidimensional collective transformative reservoir for those of the Host, e.g. Great White Brotherhood, other Planes and Dimensions, Angelic Host, and Realms and Spheres of Cherubim and

Seraphic counterparts; and we will continue until such given time to be the Translators and Mediators of Such Realm." *Articles of Faith and Constitution,* Article VI Purpose & Function, Section 3, © 1977 TE-TA-MA Truth Foundation-Family Of URI, Inc.

Online Complimentary Hyperlinks

Church Of The Creator®
churchofthecreator.com/

Church Of The Creator® Channel   YouTube
youtube.com/channel/UCvNzSVAOowNd7nOTAKf5BbQ

Priesthood Melchizedek Channel ....YouTube
youtube.com/channel/UC6BcBrLrX3T9QpcLhgne1DQ

Wikipedia Article - Church Of The Creator®
wikipedia.org/wiki/Church_of_the_Creator

APPENDIX I.

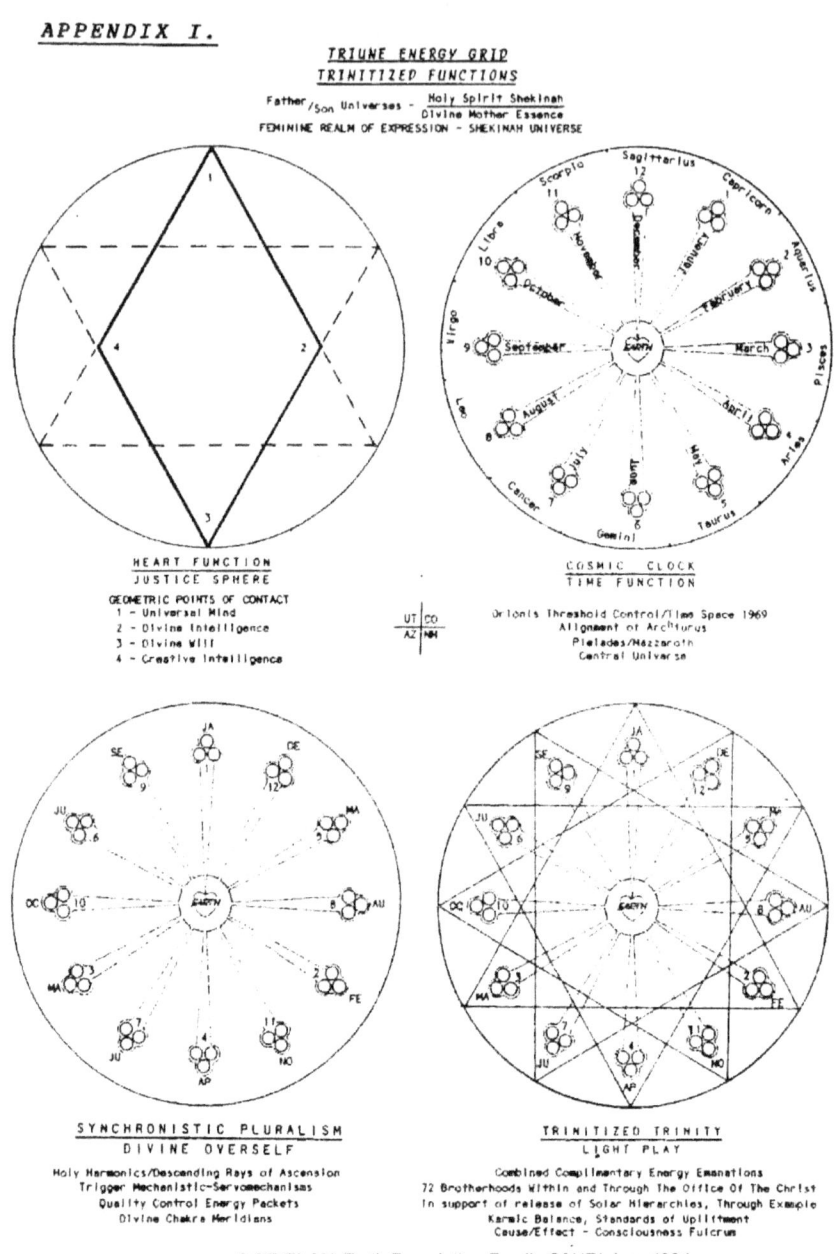

Plate 1. Triune Energy GRID - TRINITIZED FUNCTION

APPENDIX II.

ACTIVATION OF SEED CRYSTALS
THE HEART FUNCTION

THE SPIRITUAL EVALUATION AND SCIENTIFIC EQUATION OF LOVE:

$$LOVE = ME\ 16$$

M = mass/matter   E = energy

SACRED NUMEROLOGY
NUMERIC SCIENCE OUR GENETIC GRID

1	2	3	4	5	6	7	8	9	10	11	12
A-Z	B	C	D	E	F	G	H	I-J	K	L	M
N	O	P	Q	R	S	T	U	V	W	X	Y

In alignment of the 12 the 3 the ONE, the numeric-alphabetic grid for the English language.

Cosm¹o genics

Physio genics

Re-spatialization

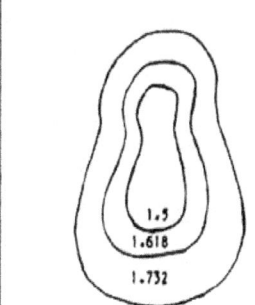

LOGARITHMIC FUNCTIONS
IN HUMANITIES' GENETIC EVOLUTION

Electronic vibratory patterns of
Biological phase-outs

Chakra - Spinpoints & meridians

© TE-TA-MA Truth Foundation-Family Of URI, Inc. 1984

Plate 2.   ACTIVATION OF SEED CRYSTALS - THE HEART FUNCTION

www.ingramcontent.com/pod-product-compliance
Lightning Source LLC
LaVergne TN
LVHW021617080426
835510LV00019B/2620